Most of the shadows of this life are caused by standing in one's own sunshine.

— Ralph Waldo Emerson

Blue Mountain Arts®

Bestselling Books

By Susan Polis Schutz:
To My Daughter, with Love, on the Important Things in Life
To My Son, with Love
I Love You

100 Things to Always Remember... and One Thing to Never Forget
by Alin Austin

Is It Time to Make a Change?
by Deanna Beisser

Trust in Yourself
by Donna Fargo

To the One Person I Consider to Be My Soul Mate
by D. Pagels

For You, Just Because You're Very Special to Me
by Collin McCarty

Chasing Away the Clouds
by Douglas Pagels

Anthologies:
42 Gifts I'd Like to Give to You
Always Believe in Yourself and Your Dreams
Creeds of Life, Love, & Inspiration
Follow Your Dreams Wherever They Lead You
For You, My Daughter
Friends Are Forever
Friends for Life
I Love You, Mom
I'm Glad You Are My Sister
The Joys and Challenges of Motherhood
The Language of Recovery ...and Living Life One Day at a Time
Life Can Be Hard Sometimes ...but It's Going to Be Okay
Marriage Is a Promise of Love
May You Always Have an Angel by Your Side
Mottos to Live By
Take Each Day One Step at a Time
Teaching and Learning Are Lifelong Journeys
There Is Greatness Within You, My Son
These Are the Gifts I'd Like to Give to You
Thoughts of Friendship
Thoughts to Share with a Wonderful Teenager
To My Child
True Friends Always Remain in Each Other's Heart
With God by Your Side ...You Never Have to Be Alone
Words of Love
You're Just like a Sister to Me

Think
Positive Thoughts
Every Day

Words to Inspire
a Brighter Outlook on Life

Edited by
Patricia Wayant

Blue Mountain Press™

SPS Studios, Inc., Boulder, Colorado

We wish to thank Susan Polis Schutz for permission to reprint the following poems that appear in this publication: "Find Happiness in Everything You Do" and "Positive Thinkers Have Twelve Qualities in Common." Copyright © 1983, 1986 by Stephen Schutz and Susan Polis Schutz. All rights reserved.

Library of Congress Catalog Card Number: 2001005101
ISBN: 0-88396-607-7

ACKNOWLEDGMENTS appear on page 64.

Certain trademarks are used under license.

Manufactured in China
First printing in hardcover: October 2001

 This book is printed on recycled paper.

This book is printed on fine quality, laid embossed, 80 lb. paper. This paper has been specially produced to be acid free (neutral pH) and contains no groundwood or unbleached pulp. It conforms with all the requirements of the American National Standards Institute, Inc., so as to ensure that this book will last and be enjoyed by future generations.

Library of Congress Cataloging-in-Publication Data

Think positive thoughts every day : words to inspire a brighter outlook on life / edited by Patricia Wayant.
        p. cm.
    ISBN 0-88396-607-7 (alk. paper)
    1. Self-realization—Quotations, maxims, etc. 2. Self-realization—Poetry. 3. Conduct of life—Quotations, maxims, etc. 4. Conduct of life—Poetry. I. Wayant, Patricia, 1953-
    PN6084.S45 T49 2001
    158.1—dc21

2001005101
CIP

SPS Studios, Inc.

P.O. Box 4549, Boulder, Colorado 80306

Contents

May You Always Have Positive Thoughts

May every day of your life bring you fresh hopes for tomorrow — because hope gives all of us our reason for trying.

May each new day bring a feeling of excitement, joy, and a wonderful sense of expectation. Expect the best, and you'll get it.

May you find peace in simple things, because those are the ones that will always be there.

May you remember the good times and forget the sorrow and pain, for the good times will remind you of how special your life has been.

May you always feel secure and loved, and know you are the best.

May you experience all the good things in life — the happiness of realizing your dreams, the joy of feeling worthwhile, and the satisfaction of knowing you've succeeded.

May you find warmth in others, expressions of love and kindness, smiles that encourage you, and friends who are loyal and honest.

May you realize the importance of patience and accept others for what they are. With understanding and love, you'll find the good in every heart.

May you have faith in others and the ability to be vulnerable. Open your heart and really share the miracle of love and intimacy.

Above all, may you always have positive thoughts.

— Regina Hill

Motto for a Positive Outlook

Refuse to be unhappy;
   be cheerful instead.
Refuse to let your troubles multiply;
   just take them one by one.
Organize your time; keep your life simple
   and exactly the way you want it.
Refuse to complain about things;
   learn to improve your surroundings
and create your world
   the way you believe it should be.
Refuse to dwell on the mistakes
   or disappointments
that are sometimes a part of life;
instead learn how you can
   make things better.
Be optimistic.
Be energetic and positive
   about the things you do,
and always hope for the best.
Believe in yourself at all times
   and in all aspects of your life.
Before you know it,
those wonderful dreams
you have believed in all your life
   will come true,
and your life will be
the happy and successful life
   that it was meant to be.

— Ben Daniels

Carry with You These Gifts
of the Heart...

Trust... that whatever happens,
   there is someone who will
      understand.
Honesty... the feeling that you
   never need to hold back.
Peace... in being accepted for
   who you really are.
Beauty... in outlook
   more than appearance.
Freedom... to be yourself,
   to change, and to grow.
Joy... in every day, in every memory,
   and in your hopes for
      the future.
Love... to last a lifetime,
   and perhaps beyond.

— D. L. Riepl

Ten Suggestions for a Brighter Future

1. Realize that life isn't always fair. Accept what you must, and change what you can.

2. Think before you act. A moment of carelessness or anger can cause years of anguish and regret.

3. Look for the beauty in life, in people, in nature, and in yourself.

4. Appreciate what you have: the people, the opportunities, the material possessions.

5. Make the effort to have fun. It's a great way to bond with others, and it makes some of the best memories.

6. Set aside some time for yourself. Do something you enjoy without feeling even a little guilty.

7. Accept others without judgment. Everyone is unique, and it's okay to be different.

8. Forgive. Bitterness and resentment hurt you more than the person you direct them at.

9. Learn. Open your mind to new ideas and activities, and don't be afraid to try.

10. Dream. Make plans, believe in yourself, and go for what you want.

— Barbara Cage

When Difficulties Arise...
"Hang In There"

Difficulties arise in the lives of us all. What is most important is dealing with the hard times, coping with the changes, and getting through to the other side where the sun is still shining just for you.

It takes a strong person to deal with tough times and difficult choices. But you are a strong person. It takes courage. But you possess the inner courage to see you through. It takes being an active participant in your life. But you are in the driver's seat, and you can determine the direction you want tomorrow to go in.

Hang in there... and take care to see
that you don't lose sight of the one
thing that is constant, beautiful, and
true: Everything will be fine — and it
will turn out that way because of the
special kind of person you are.

So... beginning today and lasting a
lifetime through — Hang in there,
and don't be afraid to feel like the
morning sun is shining... just for you.

— Douglas Pagels

Look on the Bright Side

When life seems overwhelming
and you can't seem to get
everything done...
When there isn't enough time
to relax and enjoy...
When there is little reward
for all your efforts and
you wonder if it's all worth it,
if this is what life is all about,
and if this is what the future
holds in store...

Try to keep a positive attitude by looking
for the little blessings that happen
every day yet often go unnoticed.
Keep your mind open to humorous situations,
because humor can rescue you
from being overwhelmed.
And never forget that there are people
who love and care about you;
people who want to help and support you
through life's difficult times;
people who think you're pretty special;
people who care a whole lot about you.

— Barbara Cage

Promise Yourself
Only the Best

Promise yourself
to dream more and hesitate less.
To believe in yourself more
and judge yourself less by
the accomplishments of others.
To appreciate your family
and friends
for all the wonderful ways
they make your life better.
Promise yourself
to accept life as it comes
and truly make each day special.
To become more independent
and more willing to change.
To fill your life
with special times,
and make your dreams come true.

— Deanna Beisser

Think Positive Thoughts Every Day

If your life feels like it is lacking the power that you want and the motivation that you need, sometimes all you have to do is shift your point of view.

By training your thoughts to concentrate on the bright side of things, you are more likely to have the incentive to follow through on your goals. You are less likely to be held back by negative ideas that might limit your performance.

Your life can be enhanced, and your happiness enriched, when you choose to change your perspective. Don't leave your future to chance or wait for things to get better mysteriously on their own. You must go in the direction of your hopes and aspirations. Begin to build your confidence, and work through problems rather than avoid them. Remember that power is not necessarily control over situations, but the ability to deal with whatever comes your way.

Always believe that good things are possible, and remember that mistakes can be lessons that lead to discoveries. Take your fear and transform it into trust; learn to rise above anxiety and doubt. Turn your "worry hours" into "productive hours." Take the energy that you have wasted and direct it toward every worthwhile effort that you can be involved in. You will see beautiful things happen when you allow yourself to experience the joys of life. You will find happiness when you adopt positive thinking into your daily routine and make it an important part of your world.

— Kelly D. Caron

Positive thinking is a habit, like any other; we can practice it every day until it becomes second nature to us — and along the way, transform our lives.

— Washington L. Crowley

There is nothing either good or bad, but thinking makes it so.

— William Shakespeare

Positive Thinkers Have
Twelve Qualities in Common

They have confidence in themselves
They have a very strong sense of purpose
They never have excuses for not doing something
They always try their hardest for perfection
They never consider the idea of failing
They work extremely hard towards their goals
They know who they are
They understand their weaknesses as well as their
    strong points
They can accept and benefit from criticism
They know when to defend what they are doing
They are creative
They are not afraid to be a little different in
    finding innovative solutions that will enable
        them to achieve their dreams

— Susan Polis Schutz

ALWAYS KEEP A DREAM IN YOUR HEART

If you have a dream, then — by all means —
   do what it takes to make it come true.
If you have a goal, make it something
   you strive to accomplish.
If you have a hope, then hope for it
   with all your heart.

— Collin McCarty

Hold fast your dreams!
Within your heart
Keep one still, secret spot
Where dreams may go,
And, sheltered so,
May thrive and grow
Where doubt and fear are not.
O keep a place apart,
Within your heart,
For little dreams to go!

— Louise Driscoll

Do What Makes You Happy

If you're feeling a little anxious
   as to which way to go in your life,
Take some time for yourself;
   get away someplace.
Let yourself go, set yourself free.
Look deep into your soul and ask yourself
   what would really make you happy.
Don't go in a certain direction because
   you feel you have to
Or because you planned on it for years;
Sometimes it takes a long time to know
   what you want.
Go for a long walk, sit by a fire,
   gaze out over a lake;
Go where you will find some inspiration.
Try a few different things.
Finding out what you were meant to do
   isn't about how much money you could make
   or who you might please.
You have to please yourself first;
   you have to love yourself enough to seek out
   that which gives you the most pleasure.
Eventually you will find what makes you happy.
It is worth the time that it takes to find it;
   you are worth the time.

— Carol Howard

LIVE A LIFE OF HAPPINESS

Happiness cannot come from without.
It must come from within. It is not what we
see and touch or that which others do for
us which makes us happy; it is that which
we think and feel and do, first for the
other fellow and then for ourselves.

— Helen Keller

Live so that you are at ease,
in harmony with the world,
and full of joy.

— Confucius

Joy is not in things, it is in us.

— Richard Wagner

True happiness must come from within you.
You will find happiness by letting
your conscience guide you —
listen to it; follow it.
Your conscience is the key to your happiness.

— Karen Poynter Taylor

If you can sit at set of sun
And count the deeds that you have done
      And counting find
One self-denying act, one word
That eased the heart of him that heard —
      One glance most kind,
Which fell like sunshine where he went,
Then you may count that day well spent.

— Robert Browning

Find Something to Be Grateful for Every Day

Every day, be full of awareness
of the beauty around you.
Be full of gratitude
for friends and family,
for the goodness you find in others,
for your health and all you're capable of.
Be full of acceptance
of yourself and others —
without conditions or judging,
knowing that differences and changes
make life interesting.
Appreciate the gifts of laughter
and fun in your life,
and find contentment in knowing
that you can always control
your ability to look on the bright side.

— Barbara Cage

There is nothing which can hinder or
circumvent a strong and determined
soul seeking for health, usefulness,
truth and success.

Keep that fact well in mind and live to
it, no matter what the whole world may
say to the contrary. Fear nothing. You
are a part of the splendid universe,
and you are here to get the best out
of this phase of life.... Look for
something to be thankful and glad
over each day, and you will find it....

Fill your soul and mind full of love
    and sympathy and joy...
        and blessings
        will follow.
                        — Ella Wheeler Wilcox

The happiest people in the world are those
who have a hard time recalling their worries...
and an easy time remembering their blessings.
                        — Alin Austin

Do Not Regret Your Past;
Learn from It

Far away in the distant past
lies the thought of the things
    that once were
and how they have affected
    who we are today.
We regret the things we did not do
and wish that we could change
    the things we did wrong.
We should look to the future instead.

We end up wasting our lives in remorse,
and pass right by all the good things
that are happening in the present.
If we look toward the future,
we are sure to find
at least some happiness that
will make our lives worthwhile.

You can find comfort
in the thoughts and actions
of the ones around you.
They will help you
get through the rough times
and also rejoice with you
when things are good.

Just look for the brighter days,
and you will get through life.
Many complications may arise,
and things will seem wrong,
but stick to your virtues.
Hold your head up high
so the whole world can see
    how special you are...
and you will make it.

— Lauren Hall

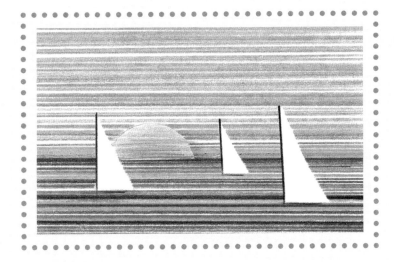

Make Each Day a New Beginning

Finish every day and be done with it. You
have done what you could. Some blunders
and absurdities no doubt crept in; forget
them as soon as you can. Tomorrow is a
new day; begin it well and serenely and
with too high a spirit to be cumbered with
your old nonsense. This day is all that
is good and fair. It is too dear, with its
hopes and invitations, to waste a moment
on the yesterdays.

— Ralph Waldo Emerson

Try to keep your soul young
and vibrant all your days
and to imagine always
...that life is only beginning.

I think that is the only way to
keep adding to one's abilities,
one's affections, and one's
inner happiness.

— George Sand

Everyday Miracles

Each day is filled with miracles
that seem so commonplace
that we sometimes forget to pause
and appreciate the wonder
    of the moment.

With every new child that's born,
each rainbow that shines,
and all the smiles we share —
a miracle is created.

People sometimes forget that miracles
are not just spectacular events
that happen once in a lifetime.
Most miracles are smaller.
The best ones of all are those
that happen every day
and reflect love and hope
for nature and humanity.

Never forget to rejoice in
each small joy...
if you celebrate only
the most spectacular events,
you'll spend a lot of time
waiting for happiness to find you.
It is best if you find the happiness.

— Patty J. Rice

Promise To...

Be kind to yourself.
Look in the mirror and see
that you are beautiful.
Make three wishes.
Be strong.
Nurture your soul.
Continue your prayers.
Let go of any pain.
Banish any anger.
Take one moment at a time.
Hear music.
Make music.
Seek inspiration.
Learn.
Believe in fairy tales
and in the magic
of your dreams.
Find that dreams do come true.
Hug yourself.
Feel the sun shine.
Believe again.
Smile.
Seek laughter.
Always remember that you have
a guardian angel
watching over you.
Find hope.
Find your true love.

— Linda Ann McConnell

Be glad of life
because it gives you the chance
to love
and to work
and to play
and to look at the stars.

— Henry Van Dyke

Keep your face
to the sunshine
and you cannot
see the shadow.

— Helen Keller

Keep On Believing!

Keep believing that you have
   what it takes
to make your dream
   into a reality.
Keep thinking positive thoughts,
and know that you have the ability
   to do anything.
Find the encouragement
   inside yourself
to know that you're worthwhile
   and distinct —
someone who deserves
   the very best there is.

Keep on trying.
Accept those things that you must,
change the things that are the worst,
and learn to find security and peace
    within your heart, your strength,
        and your self-assurance.
Keep on being the person
    that you are —
the one who gives those around you
such a feeling of reassurance and hope.
Keep on believing, because you deserve
the joy, peace, faith, hope, and love
that you're seeking.
You deserve every fulfillment
and satisfaction in everything you try.

— Regina Hill

Never Give Up Hope

Life doesn't always give us
    the joys we want.
We don't always get our hopes
    and dreams,
and we don't always get
    our own way.
But don't give up hope,
because you can make a difference
one situation and one person
    at a time.

Look for the beauty around you —
in nature, in others, in yourself —
and believe in the love
of friends, family, and humankind.

You can find love in a smile
    or a helping hand,
in a thoughtful gesture
    or a kind word.
It is all around, if you
    just look for it.

Give love,
for in giving it
you will find the power in life
along with the joy, happiness,
patience, and understanding.

Believe in the goodness of others
and remember that anger
    and depression
can be countered by love and hope.

Even when you feel as though
there isn't a lot you can do
to change unhappiness or problems,
you can always do a little —
and a little at a time
eventually makes a big difference.

— Barbara Cage

How to Grow Happiness

Step 1:

Plant yourself deep in a bed of faith,
and pack it down solid and tight. Drench
daily with positive thinking, and keep
saturated just right. Mulch often with
forgiveness, for this will help you grow.

Quickly remove any seeds of worry,
for they will soon germinate, and keep
out the weeds of despair. Nourish
disappointments with hope whenever it is
needed, and always stay cool and shaded
when you feel irritated or heated. Trim
away guilt and depression, for they create
decay, and cultivate with happy memories
as often as every day.

Step 2:

Harvest the lessons of the past; just
dig, pick, and hoe. And nurture the roots
of the present, for now is when you
flourish and grow. Start planting for the
future; set your goals in a row. Spade
the bed well for all your dreams to grow.

Step 3:

Remember that grief is a natural predator, so learn to tolerate some damage. Protect your garden with daily prayers, for this will help you manage. Bury the criticism and complaining, for they are injurious pests.

Sow the seeds of love wherever you may go — for joy, love, and laughter are surely bound to grow. Although the thorns of life may be here to stay, just sprout a smile along the way... and be thankful for what you have today!

— Michele Rossi

Have Faith,
and Expect the Best

Faith begins
by believing
in your heart
that what is right
has a chance.

Faith is knowing
in your heart
that good can
overcome evil,
that the sun can shine
in a rainstorm.

Faith is peaceful
and comforting,
because it
comes from within
where no one
can invade
your private dreams.

Faith is not something
you can demand
or command;
it is a result of
commitment to belief.

Faith is believing
in something
you can't see or hear,
something deep inside
that only you understand
and only you control.

Faith is trusting
in yourself
enough to know
that no matter
how things turn out,
you will make
the best of them.

— Beth Fagan Quinn

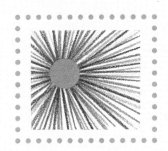

Always Be as Happy as You Possibly Can Be

Love yourself every day
and remember
how many people love you.
Do good things for others,
but also give to yourself.
Release the child within you
so you can sing,
laugh, and play.
List the things
that you do best,
and give yourself a hug.
Accept compliments.
Dance barefoot.
Plan to fulfill a secret wish.
Laugh at yourself.
And above all,
remember you are loved.

— Jacqueline Schiff

There is no difficulty that enough love will not conquer; No disease that enough love will not heal; No door that enough love will not open; No gulf that enough love will not bridge; No wall that enough love will not throw down; No sin that enough love will not redeem.

It makes no difference how deeply seated may be the trouble; How hopeless the outlook; How muddled the tangle; How great the mistake. A sufficient realization of love will dissolve it all... If you only could love enough you would be the happiest and most powerful being in the world.

— Emmet Fox

A Positive Attitude
Is the Key to Success

Before you say "I can't,"
   Make sure you've already tried.
Before you let doubts stop you,
   Confront them with facts.
Before reasons convince you it's impossible,
   Pursue the one reason that
      makes it possible.
Before failure enters your mind,
   Hide success in your heart.
Before fear holds you back,
   Go forward with faith.
Before problems interfere with your plans,
   Use them to accomplish your goals.
Before you hold back because you think
      others are better,
   Show them what a winner you are.
Before you settle for less,
   Hold on to what is most important.
Before you believe there is no way,
   Keep going and you'll make one.
Before you give up,
   Be at peace inside.
Before you dismiss your dreams,
   Wait until they've come true.
Before you go looking for happiness,
   Make your own where you are!

— Nancye Sims

Hope

Hope is not the closing of your eyes
　　to the difficulty, the risk,
　　or the failure.

It is a trust that —
　　if I fail now —
　　I shall not fail forever;
　　and if I am hurt,
　　　I shall be healed.

It is a trust that
　　life is good,
　　love is powerful,
　　and the future is full of promise.

　　　　　　　　　　　　— Anonymous

Ten Things to Remember
When Your Feelings
Have Been Trampled On

1. Whether it's a family member, somebody at work, or your best friend who's hurt you badly, put yourself in their shoes and treat them the way you would want to be treated, even if they don't deserve it.

2. If you've heard something you didn't want to hear, remember it may not be 100% true. So lighten up. If it's not urgent, put off thinking about it for a couple of days. Forgive the person who wronged you; don't forget, you're doing this for yourself, too. Prove to yourself that you can practice what you believe. Try to be as understanding of others as you would want them to be of you.

3. There will always be losers and winners. Act according to how you want to feel about yourself when all is said and done. Don't judge what others do if you don't want them to judge you.

4. Remember, what other people do is their responsibility. Don't let them cause you to carry a grudge and let their actions weigh you down. They are not responsible for your actions, no matter what they do. You are.

5. If someone has said something untrue about you or done something intentionally to hurt you, wish good things for that person — even if you don't feel like it. Ask for them what you desire for yourself, and it will draw those things to you.

6. If you've made a mistake or disappointed yourself or others, apologize quickly and earnestly; that's all you can do. Let your remorse teach you how to have compassion for others when they make mistakes. Nobody's perfect, even though we all try to be. If someone can't accept your apology, that's okay, too. Just do the right thing and go on.

7. Talk less and listen more; you could learn something about others and about yourself. If you feel like yelling, go outside and throw rocks on the cement instead. Take a walk or, better yet, sing... it will put a melody back in your life.

8. If you think someone is making fun of you or someone you love, disarm them, not with your fist, but with your best smile. Give them something they don't know how to give. Speak to them; be bold. Ask that they be blessed and you'll be blessed, too. Forgiveness is a powerful thing; it will help your body and soul. Don't let anyone cause you to act the way they've acted toward you, and remember that they have a right to do whatever they choose also.

9. Don't hide your hurts and pains and feelings inside where they will harden your heart. Use common sense and understanding to process them. Don't react just from your feelings; respond with maturity rather than childish habit. You won't regret it.

10. Get in touch with the person you want to be and become that. Listen to your heart... you can find the answer there to every question you have. Remember, no matter how you're treated, just treat others the way you would want to be treated when your feelings are getting trampled on.

— Donna Fargo

Forgiveness

Forgiveness is letting go of the pain
and accepting what has happened
because it will not change.

Forgiveness is dismissing the blame.
Choices were made that caused the hurt;
we each could have chosen differently,
but we didn't.

Forgiveness is looking at the pain,
learning the lessons it has produced,
and understanding what we have learned.

Forgiveness allows us to move on
toward a better understanding
of universal love
and our true purpose.

Forgiveness is knowing that love
is the answer to all questions
and that we all
are in some way connected.

Forgiveness is starting over
with the knowledge
that we have gained.
It is saying:
"I forgive you, and I forgive myself.
I hope you can do the same."

— Judith Mammay

Try to Remember
the Good Things

When times become difficult
(and you know they sometimes will),
remember a moment in your life
that was filled with joy
    and happiness.
Remember how it made you feel,
and you will have the strength
    you need
to get through any trial.

When life throws you
    one more obstacle
than you think you can handle,
remember something you achieved
through perseverance
and by struggling to the end.
In doing so, you'll find
you have the ability to overcome
each obstacle brought your way.

When you find yourself drained
and depleted of energy,
remember to find a place
    of sanctuary and rest.
Take the necessary time
    in your own life
to dream your dreams
and renew your energy,
so you'll be ready to face
    each new day.

When you feel tension building,
find something fun to do.
You'll find that the stress you feel
    will dissipate
and your thoughts
    will become clearer.

When you're faced with
so many negative
    and draining situations,
realize how minuscule
    problems will seem
when you view your life as a whole —
and remember the positive things.

— Sherrie L. Householder

It's easy to look on the
    bright side of things
    when all is going well...
    when the smiles outweigh the frowns
    and the sunshine is streaming
      in the window.
But the happiest people
    are the ones who can say —
    when all is going wrong,
    when the clouds get in the way —
    that a little unhappiness
    must balance the joys,
    and that a bit of sadness
    has its place in the world, too.
For they know, these special people,
    of the balance of nature's ways.
    They know that nothing grows
    where the sun always shines,
    and that gray skies and rain
    can be an unregrettable
      sign of the day.
For these fortunate people,
    their favorite season
    is always the one they are in,
    and they continue to look
    on the bright side,
    knowing that the sunshine
      might leave for a while,
    but that it will
    never be gone
    for long.
                            — Jamie Delere

There has not been a single day since the
world began when the sun was not shining.
The trouble has been with our vision.

— Anonymous

Most of the shadows of this life are
caused by standing in one's own sunshine.

— Ralph Waldo Emerson

A single sunbeam is enough
to drive away any shadows.

— Saint Francis of Assisi

The Keys to a Positive Perspective...

Happiness, as much as your heart can hold
An abundance of laughter
Patience with the loved ones in your life
   and with your own shortcomings
Yesterdays that comfort you
   and promise you better tomorrows
Faith in yourself and your goals
Reassuring smiles to warm your days
Heart-healing hugs to sustain you
   through any tears
Dreams that lead you forward and
   help you grow
Acceptance when you sometimes fail
Determination to try again and again
Courage to go on when you are afraid
Warmth when it's cold outside
A star when the night is dark
The wings of a butterfly
The heart of a songbird
And, always, a rainbow
   after every storm

— Vickie M. Worsham

Don't Ever Lose Faith
in Yourself

Never think that any part of you
Is lacking.
Never doubt your abilities.
Never question your judgment.
Never let anyone or anything
Make you feel less than you are,
Because who you are
   Is someone special.

Never feel that the next step
Is a step too far.
If you're stumbling as you walk,
Hold your head high and
Know that no other person's
Words or actions
Can ever hurt you,
Because who you are
   Is someone special.

Never lose faith in yourself.
Just look around you —
At the friends who surround you —
Because they love and care for you,
Support you,
And believe in you...
   Because you are someone special.

             — Ashley Bell

Believe that
You Can Do Anything,
and You Will!

Imagine yourself to be the type of person you want to be, and then be it. You may have to let go of some bad habits and develop some more positive ones, but don't give up — for it is only in trying and persisting that dreams come true.

Expect changes to occur, and realize that the power to make those changes comes from within you. Your thoughts and actions, your choices and decisions, and the way you spend your time determine who you are and who you will become.

You are capable and worthy of being and doing anything. You just need the discipline and determination to see it through. It won't come instantly, and you may backslide from time to time, but don't let that deter you. Never give up.

Life is an ever-changing process, and nothing is final. Therefore, each moment and every new day is a chance to begin anew.

— Barbara Cage

You Can
Make Something Happy
Out of Everything That
Happens in Life

Life can make choices for us.
Sometimes these choices
    seem unhappy or unfair,
but in the end we control
our own destiny because we can decide
    how people and events affect us.

So much of our happiness lies within
    the choices that we make.
We can accept that life
    isn't the way we want it to be,
    or we can change it so that it will be.

We can walk through the shadows,
　　or we can choose to smile
　　and seek out the sunlight.
We can create grand dreams
　　that never leave the ground,
　　or we can be builders of dreams that come true.
We can look at only
　　the negative aspects of ourselves,
　　or we can lift ourselves up
　　by being our own best friend.
We can live in the past
　　or dream about the future,
　　or we can live for today.
We can give up when the road becomes difficult,
　　or we can keep on going
　　until the view is much better.
The choices in life are endless,
　　and so is the potential for happiness.

— Nancye Sims

Let Your Positive Side Shine

Always hold honor as a high virtue.
Despite how the world may be,
rise above.
Always speak the truth, because others
will hold you in high esteem as a
person who can be trusted.
Never lose faith in your fellow human
beings, despite times when they may
let you down.
Believe in hard work. No one will hand
you the future you want. The ladder
to success is steep, but take one step
at a time and you'll get to the top.
Always believe in yourself. Your happiness
depends on no one else but you.
If there is something that you are
unhappy about, you must change it.
Always hold love close to you. When you
make a commitment, cherish it for the
rest of your life.

— Sherrie L. Householder

Find Happiness
in Everything You Do

Find happiness in nature
in the beauty of a mountain
in the serenity of the sea
Find happiness in friendship
in the fun of doing things together
in the sharing and understanding
Find happiness in your family
in the stability of knowing
    that someone cares
in the strength of love and honesty
Find happiness in yourself
in your mind and body
in your values and achievements
Find happiness in
everything
you
do

— Susan Polis Schutz

Make Every Day Special

Be thankful and look to every new day with positive hope.

Take time to pull yourself away from all the noise and just look around you. Take inventory. Appreciate those who have enhanced the quality of your life, and remember that they have been a gift to you. Also remember that you're a gift to them, too.

Be grateful for the choices you've made, both good and bad. Accept your mistakes; you can't change them anyway. Apply what you've learned and go on. Use these lessons to help you with your other decisions in life. Appreciate yourself and your own uniqueness.

Go outside and look at the sky.
Soak in the atmosphere. Enjoy the
colors of the landscape. Feel the
textures of every place you are that
you're thankful for. Smile at the world.
Don't allow any negative feelings to
creep into your consciousness. Feel
the power of your own acceptance.
Put a positive spin on every thought
you have.

Make every day special. Own it.
Enjoy it. Bask in the glory of life.
Appreciate the gift of your own life.

— Donna Fargo

Most of All...
Be Happy!

Always see the goodness in this world,
do your part in helping those
  less fortunate,
walk hand in hand with those
  of less talent,
follow those of more knowledge,
and be an equal with those
  who are different.
Find your special purpose
  in this world so full of choices
and help lead those who stray.
Become your own individual —
set yourself apart from those who
  are the same.

Have the self-confidence to say no
    when it is necessary
and the strength to stand alone.
Give yourself the approval
    to love and respect everything that
        you are and will become.
Reap the fruits of your talents,
walk with pride down the road of life,
be humble in your successes,
and share in the praises and joy of others.
Most of all, be happy.
For when you are happy,
    you have the key that will open all
        of the world's doors to you.

                                    — Jackie Olson

ACKNOWLEDGMENTS

The following is a partial list of authors whom the publisher especially wishes to thank for permission to reprint their works.

Barbara Cage for "Ten Suggestions for a Brighter Future," "Look on the Bright Side," and "Never Give Up Hope." Copyright © 1998 by Barbara Cage. All rights reserved.

Kelly D. Caron for "Think Positive Thoughts Every Day." Copyright © 1998 by Kelly D. Caron. All rights reserved.

Carol Howard for "Do What Makes You Happy." Copyright © 2001 by Carol Howard. All rights reserved.

Lauren Hall for "Do Not Regret Your Past; Learn from It." Copyright © 2001 by Lauren Hall. All rights reserved.

Patty J. Rice for "Everyday Miracles." Copyright © 2001 by Patty J. Rice. All rights reserved.

Linda Ann McConnell for "Promise To...." Copyright © 1998 by Linda Ann McConnell. All rights reserved.

Regina Hill for "Keep On Believing!" Copyright © 1998 by Regina Hill. All rights reserved.

Michele Rossi for "How to Grow Happiness." Copyright © 1998 by Michele Rossi. All rights reserved.

Beth Fagan Quinn for "Have Faith, and Expect the Best." Copyright © 1998 by Beth Fagan Quinn. All rights reserved.

Nancye Sims for "A Positive Attitude Is the Key to Success." Copyright © 1998 by Nancye Sims. All rights reserved.

PrimaDonna Entertainment Corp. for "Ten Things to Remember..." and "Make Every Day Special" by Donna Fargo. Copyright © 1998 by PrimaDonna Entertainment Corp. All rights reserved.

Sherrie L. Householder for "Try to Remember the Good Things." Copyright © 1998 by Sherrie L. Householder. All rights reserved.

Vickie M. Worsham for "The Keys to a Positive Perspective...." Copyright © 1998 by Vickie M. Worsham. All rights reserved.

Ashley Bell for "Don't Ever Lose Faith in Yourself." Copyright © 1998 by Ashley Bell. All rights reserved.

A careful effort has been made to trace the ownership of poems used in this anthology in order to obtain permission to reprint copyrighted materials and give proper credit to the copyright owners. If any error or omission has occurred, it is completely inadvertent, and we would like to make corrections in future editions provided that written notification is made to the publisher:

SPS Studios, Inc., P.O. Box 4549, Boulder, Colorado 80306.